INSIGHTS WITHOUT SOUND

Angela Rogers

INSIGHTS WITHOUT SOUND

A Deaf Christian's Journey to Understand
God and Life as told through Her Own Eyes

ANGELA ROGERS

Foreword

Dear reader,

I never thought I would be a writer for this first book. I had an older sister and mother who wrote several books before I was adopted at three years old from China. My older sister wrote a brief autobiography about our family, mainly about her service dog, a Black Labrador named Chloe.

Still, I wrote this book hoping that my words and realizations on life may offer some comfort and realization for readers like you. I have some relatable experiences, and you may be curious to see a bit of my Deaf world and how my beliefs in Jesus Christ fit into my life. I pray that you read it with an open mind and open heart. I am not forcing or compelling you to believe in God. It is a free will that God gives us, a choice to believe in His Son or follow our desires. Please read the book with an open mind and leave with some things to consider.

To share briefly, I am a Deaf Chinese adoptee, and I grew up in an international and bilingual family. I was in mainstream schools until I entered Gallaudet University in 2016 due to my primary focus on better education. It was an extraordinary experience being in the Deaf world in the university in a literal sense. I grew to appreciate my Deaf identity and discovered my values throughout my life. My values are faith, open-mindedness, and a growth mindset. Faith is the anchor and the reason I keep going instead of giving up, and open-mindedness is something I strive to utilize because judgment is not what humans have a right to have. We do not know what is in other people's lives or why they act in a certain way. Still, judgment is not reserved for us to act on to determine our social standing in society. Judgment is only reserved for God because He is omnipresent and makes wise judgments. The growth mindset allows me to change and improve myself as I want to present my best self, facing God when I die, knowing that I did my best in this life.

Now, after you read my book, it will change your perspective on life a bit differently and help you grow to appreciate your pace in life as well. With that note, enjoy the reading and remember life is a gift from God even if you do not believe in Him!

Table of Contents

1

Knowledge Is Important,
But Wisdom Is Far Better

"Why are people so fascinated with mystery, I ask? The wise man answers, 'well, they prefer to know than not know.' A thirst for knowledge or to quench their curiosity?"

As far as I know, the mystery has existed for centuries and never disappeared. People love to understand to satisfy their curiosities. It is part of our human DNA to seek out what we can find and solve things beyond our understanding. Inquisitiveness is good because it increases our desire for knowledge and expands our learning capabilities as we explore possibilities. That is why many distinguished people in our history achieved their ambitions and dreams. They allowed their desire for knowledge to grow. People are incredible when they succeed by letting their curious selves shine in any area of life.

I wrote this quote to express my understanding of life and why people question things, in general, to understand why it happens to satisfy their curiosity. It is good to be curious, but it is best to be cautious and to know where they should avoid crossing the lines. Otherwise, they will be in deep waters because they need more time to learn that information. Nevertheless, knowledge is essential to fight against the foolishness and oppression we see around us.

A bible verse came to my mind when I was writing this chapter. ***"The prudent see danger and take refuge, but the simple keep going and pay the penalty" (Proverbs 22:3)*** provides an idea of how a person should use this verse daily. If people follow this advice, they will live long lives with fewer worries and cares. You may not want to take advice from religious books or word of kind advice from religious people; regardless of that, everyone should commonly hear this advice around the world. Think of your parents, teachers, mentors, coaches, and friends who may scold you if you did something wrong and tell you advice similar to the bible verse. Then it is something that you need to heed and keep in your heart as you go through your life. Therefore, I encourage you to make wise or right decisions even if it is not easy, despite others saying it is okay to do this or that. Pause and think if it is correct or not, then follow that decision you have made. For example, in January 2023, I was that "simple" one who made a stupid decision to turn left when the green light was on. Still, I should see if the coast was clear before turning. It was a humbling experience that I should be prudent instead of making an impulsive decision that concluded in a terrible ending: discovering that the car was totaled. I had to use the metro to commute for a while. On the other hand, it was not due to spiritual warfare or Satan's action. I realized it was God's loving rebuke to recognize my sins and make necessary changes internally or how I should live my life.

I confessed that I am not a perfect Christian as people imagined Christians should be. I am not proud of things that I did in the past or even in the present, but I know that I am working on improving myself with the help of my Lord Jesus Christ. These lessons from my horrible experiences were valuable experiences I will always carry. They reminded me to strive to be a woman of God and consider what Jesus would do in each situation. Sometimes I forget what Jesus would do and make my own decision instead of looking to God for help. Of course, I started to experience more turns and detours after making my own decision. I urge people not to make stereotypes when they meet Christians, such as the commonly heard words, hypocrite, and to see that Christians call themselves because they show that they need God. That is something vulnerable in declaring that they need and lean on God to guide them, and that, my friend, shows bravery and courage in confessing they need help. They are not ashamed to admit that fact.

There is an excellent biblical verse that everyone, including myself, should practice, even atheists and non-religious believers because they should receive this similar advice everywhere in their every sphere of life. 1 Thessalonians 4:11 states you should ***"...make it your ambition to lead a quiet life: You should mind your own business and work with your hands, just as we told you,"*** pretty much tells us that we should focus on our lanes and not be involved in other people's business and just work to earn food on our tables. Sometimes people do not get the memo, and it just causes a lot of chaos and frustration in our lives. I did experience some similar experiences where I wish people would stop being so nosy and concerned about my business. At the same time, they should stay in their lanes and focus on their life. I have started to appreciate peace even more. I have a more profound desire to live a quiet and peaceful life where people do not bother me or cause me more frustration than necessary. However, I remember that God sometimes puts these people in our lives to teach us something or understand a valuable lesson He wants us to realize.

Thus, keep your curiosity healthy instead of one that will lead you to the deep end, where you cannot get out and experience more chaos than you want in your life. Be sure to stop and think if it is just a curiosity or something else than curiosity, then recognize it and make a wise decision from there. Otherwise, you will not realize that more troubles will come your way if you choose to pursue your curiosity.

Even so, I remain open-minded and strive to listen and be empathetic to other people's stories like Jesus did when he encountered different kinds of people in his travels with his disciplines. He intends to teach kindness and humanity in his travels so his disciples can learn and practice that when they start their ministry. That is something that Christians and I strive to be like Jesus. Just listen and be empathetic because that shows love to people. Love has different ways for people to act, and listening is one of them.

Knowledge is something that people can use to help others to make their life better and acknowledge that we cannot always know everything or be able to comprehend things that are beyond our understanding. Additionally, open-mindedness helps me increase my knowledge by hearing people's stories and learning in schools. Knowledge is essential, but wisdom is gained from knowledge and allows us to make informed and careful choices. Consider this verse about wisdom:
"Is not wisdom found among the aged? Does not long life bring understanding? To God belong wisdom and power; counsel and understanding are his" (Job 12:12-13).

Angela Rogers

2

Humility Teaches Us
More Than Our Ego Does

*"A fool can be wise sometimes, but a wise one
becomes a fool for a certain reason."*

I have been reading Chinese and Korean novels for the past few years, and their writing helped me shift my perspective on life and people in some ways. I recommend you read these novels because they guide you to view the world and people differently; I guarantee it! I grew to appreciate the depth of the story plots and the feelings they invoke when I read the highlights and surprising twists, including the wise sayings in these books. For instance, there are always one or a few foolish villains in Chinese romance, reincarnation / transmigration / rebirth, and cultivation novels. Not only that, in these genres, there are often main characters who are very clever and manage to demolish the evil plans; however, they will usually fall from grace due to commonly used tricks such as the usage of their loved ones as hostages, assassination attempts, getting involved in misunderstandings, and much more. The foolish villains surprisingly can be cunning when the action demands them to do something to get what they want regardless of the consequences or affect the main characters to fall from grace.

Reading these novels helped me realize that people can do great things. Nonetheless, they are equally capable of doing horrible things for different reasons, such as greed, power-hungry, ambition, money-chasing, fame, or a deep desire to improve their lives. In other words, the foolish ones who are greedy can be smart once or twice. At the same time, intelligent or successful people can fall for a scheme that causes them to lose everything. I have been a fool and a wise person in my life, and I am sure that everyone agrees with that because they have experienced being a foolish and wise person too.

I had been a fool for being arrogant and prideful in my pre-teens in mainstream elementary school. I was dismissive of my interpreter and ignored them when they greeted me for a while. My stupid and rude actions resulted in a consequence I would never have imagined. It brought me down very low to the point where I developed mild depression and a deeper introverted personality. I saw people, including interpreters, who were friendly to me, like saying hello to me, become so distant and obnoxious when they saw me. They whispered to each other that I had a horrible attitude in front of me, even some hearing teachers and students the same age as me a few times. It was a harsh blow to my ego and helped me realize that actions cause consequences. I realized I had done something that made me a "rude person" to everyone. Therefore, I endured the last few years of elementary school, remaining quiet and cautious of my actions. I thought I had to pay for my mistake by staying low and respectful to the point where I was a doormat to others. This horrible experience profoundly changed me to be a person who is respectful and polite to others, and I did not recognize myself where I forced myself to repress myself and to please everyone. (It took me a long time until I told myself to stop pleasing everyone because no one cares and is too focused on their life). I was in a deep depression, but I believed I had a high-functioning depression for a long time until my last year at Gallaudet University. It took me a long time until I told myself to stop dwelling on my past, including letting go of the grudges and moving on.

That was a great lesson in my foolishness, even though I was a high achiever throughout my school years. I was not very proud of what I did according to this experience. Undoubtedly, I was thankful for this lesson because I saw the ugly sides of people, including myself, and people can change to be better than before. I am living proof of this change. God did humble me, and I was very thankful because I could see that I am in the best version I wanted to be instead of this prideful, arrogant, and foolish younger self. This experience shows that even intelligent or successful people have moments of foolishness. Read the verses below and think about your experiences that deeply humble you.

> ***"For those who exalt themselves will be humbled, and those who humble themselves will be exalted." (Matthew 23:12)***

"At one time we too were foolish, disobedient, deceived and enslaved by all kinds of passions and pleasures. We lived in malice and envy, being hated and hating one another. But when the kindness and love of God our Savior appeared, he saved us, not because of righteous things we had done, but because of his mercy. He saved us through the washing of rebirth and renewal by the Holy Spirit," (Titus 3:3-5a)

"not looking to your own interests but each of you to the interests of the others. In your relationships with one another, have the same mindset as Christ Jesus:" (Philippians 2:4-5)

3

Changes Are Inevitable
in All Seasons

*"Seasons are all-changing and unpredictable.
They teach humans to appreciate the little things
and know changes are inevitable."*

I learned something after living for one-fourth of my life on Earth. Seasons only sometimes happen on time or within four months of each season. Sometimes things are slower and do not happen on time as I wish. Results do not occur in plain sight but deep inside our spirits and heart. Changes in soul and heart are profound and life-changing compared to what is happening outside our eyes. The changes inside are noteworthy compared to those outside because it demonstrates the growth and improvements in our mind and spirit. I appreciate things more when my life stagnates and moves slower than expected. They taught me to stop and enjoy the beauty around me. I started to practice patience more and have some self-reflection on what I need to improve, such as my flaws and the lessons I experienced daily.

God is trying to teach me something, and the slow seasons are His opportunity to tell me so I can finally see and ask for His help to improve that. In addition, during these slow seasons, God is working on something that prepares me for the next season. Thus, some slow seasons are considered the "season of transition" to something surprising or perhaps a new chapter of our life. God explains why seasons are different and ever-changing in this beautiful verse that summarizes why he intends them to be: ***"there is a time for everything, and a season for every activity under the heavens… a time for war and a time for peace" (Ecclesiastes 3:1-8)***. Therefore, we should face the changes bravely and fearlessly because that is what God wants us to experience and to understand that changes are not necessarily bad. We need to remember that God intends for our good and helps us to be less attracted to the secular world we live in today. God is a jealous God, and He hates it if we hold worldly things more closely than Himself. Sometimes we lose something valuable to realize that we can live without it or open our eyes to look at God more often.

Also, sometimes some seasons are the trial that God intends to test us to see if we remain faithful or fall to our temptations and desires, resulting in forgetting or forsaking God for this short-lived life on Earth. Think of this verse as you read further in this chapter: ***"And without faith it is impossible to please God, because anyone who comes to him must believe that he exists and that he rewards those who earnestly seek him" (Hebrews 11:6)***. I chose God because there is Heaven and eternal life with Jesus instead of life on Earth. Life on Earth is concise and fast when we blink our eyes. Moreover, we cannot bring our current riches and treasures after we die; therefore, there is no point in holding obsessively to earthly things. Can you answer this question: ***"What good is it for someone to gain the whole world, yet forfeit their soul?" (Mark 8:36)***. A person can have the whole world in his hands, but are they much happier this way? Think of Joseph Stalin or Hitler. They have everything, such as power, adoration, and admiration, yet their life ends unhappily. So, it is not worth pursuing earthly things that will become useless in their time. Even a legacy will fade in time. There are already more incredible treasures in Heaven awaiting us. This lesson reminds me of the story of Job, who suffered different trials by Satan but prevailed, in the end, resulting in receiving greater rewards and blessings from God, who was pleased with his faithfulness. Job refused to renounce his faith in God despite the urging from his wife and friends. I applauded this action because it was painful for him to experience physical and emotional pain by losing his family and financial resources. Despite that, he stubbornly held fast to his faith and knew he suffered for a reason, but he did not ask God why it was happening to him.

To me, Job is an example of absolute faith and endurance. I feel like I am Job in many ways because I experienced some difficult times to the point that I was deeply depressed and wanted to end my life several times. The attempts were unsuccessful, and I stopped because I felt deeply in my soul that He was telling me everything would be okay, and it was not my time to go. Also, he was telling me that He needs me here and has a big assignment for me in the future (at this point, I did not understand why He needs me here, but I realize now). Of course, I was sad and disappointed, but I chose to obey because I realized that God gave me the gift of life, and I cannot deny God's decision when it was time to take me home. Choosing obedience over my selfish desire was arduous, but I picked Him over myself, knowing it would be worth it. I intend to see what He needs me for and die satisfied knowing that I fulfill His purpose in me. Endurance is not my favorite trait, but it is part of my trait never to give up and keep going even if I do not want to. God knew I was holding on to life and waiting for His call to take me home.

That is where I deepen my appreciation and gratitude daily because life is a beautiful gift. This verse is something that everyone needs to digest: ***"If we live, we live for the Lord; and if we die, we die for the Lord. So, whether we live or die, we belong to the Lord. For this very reason, Christ died and returned to life so that he might be the Lord of both the dead and the living"*** ***(Romans 14:8-9)***. That verse is a motto that Christians, including me, use as a constant assurance that God is in control, and He is always with us to the end.

Courage

A simple truth
An unshakable belief
The hope of all kinds
The eternal faith

4

Memories Are Precious
in Our Hearts

"Once you live a moment, pause and close your eyes. In your mind, your moments live forever. Cherish them always."

People need to remember to stop and relish the moments of their life. If people keep going in their life or are too focused on one thing, they will miss out on many things. People can stop for a minute and have a flashback of a beautiful moment they experienced or share with their loved ones. These moments are why we feel so alive and understand certain emotions that come with these memories. It is a constant reminder that we are human beings with feelings and memories. We have souls that hold emotions and brains that store memories, which are intangible but very important to us. They are valuable to our existence and are why we live and breathe.

It brought up the verse to my mind that reminds me how we, the believers, will remain grateful and joyful in daily life: ***"Finally, brothers and sisters, whatever is true, whatever is noble, whatever is right, whatever is pure, whatever is lovely, whatever is admirable—if anything is excellent or praiseworthy—think about such things" (Philippians 4:8).*** It is a perfect verse that summarizes why we need to think about these beautiful memories and appreciate the bad things that come to us because God intends to change us inside instead of outside. God values what we have in ourselves instead of what we portray to the world. Life on Earth is just a taste of what Heaven will be like when we die and live with the Lord. The beautiful things we experience on Earth allow us to appreciate being alive and rejoice in God's blessings. Not only that, but He also needs us to fulfill His plan on Earth, and life experiences made us faithful prayer warriors.

I had a fantastic memory demonstrating the leap of faith in the literal sense. I visited Guam for my international internship during my first year at Gallaudet University. It was a wonderful experience being out of the country and seeing Deaf people with different perspectives and lifestyles. Anyway, I went with the other Gallaudet interns to the 45 ft or much taller cliff overlooking the surging ocean. The crag is shaped in U-shaped rock and has some foot grips for us to climb after jumping into the water near the cliff. It would be terrifying since we were at a high elevation, and the water was too deep for us to be unable to see the bottom. Most interns had already jumped into the water and had a fun time. I looked at the water and waited for the perfect time to jump because the water was surging back to the ocean, and jumping at that time was dangerous. I was waiting for the moment when water rushed straight to the middle of the U-shaped cliff – we were on the right side – and jumped when I saw it. It felt like forever when I jumped and was still in the air. It felt so surreal, like the world was moving much slower. I wrote a poem to describe precisely that surreal experience.

What is the feeling like when you are jumping from a cliff? The world is falling away, and I am standing suspended in time. Suddenly, water rushes to swallow me, splashing me into a wet reality.

It summarizes this spectacular experience, and this experience reminds me that life is short and keeps as many memories as possible in my mind. I cherished my time during this internship and my time with these interns. It was an experience I would never forget, and I certainly missed that time with them. Still, I will always carry the memories, including this one, as long as I live.

Now I want to remind you all that life is short. Live presently and enjoy every moment, even the bad times. It makes you feel alive, doesn't it? Worrying or being anxious wastes your time and does not help you. I encourage you to heed this advice because I need this daily reminder too.

Angela Rogers

5

Sorrow And Regrets
Are the Lifelong Companions

"Sorrow," they say, comes with regrets. But I refute it. No, sorrow appears when it is too late to regret."

This quote certainly brought up some painful feelings and the sense of sorrow that you experience during times of loss and painful memories. I have already experienced this similar feeling several times. We do not usually discuss it with our loved ones and colleagues. However, everyone already went through a kind of sorrow throughout their lifetime, and it is unavoidable to experience that. I am sure that we do not want to feel or experience that. It is good to realize that sorrow helps us learn our priorities in life and spend time with family and friends. We do not know that we may be gone the next day, so we should make the best of it and leave something memorable for them to remember us by or remember our loved ones.

For example, I experienced a profound loss that I will never forget, and I wished I could spend one more day with them, but it was too late. It was an unforgettable and unexpected experience for me as a young child aged about 6-8. My mother found an old couple, Sophia and

John (names changed for confidentiality), who were willing to take care of my two adopted sisters -- one hearing and one Deaf -- and me, so she dropped us off at that couple's house and went to work. We had great and fun times at the couple's home. My hearing sister had a close friendship with them; we love them too. One day, certainly out of the blue, my sisters and I got off the school bus at the couple's house and saw police cars everywhere. We were naturally bewildered at everything going on. The hearing sister had an inkling of what was happening, but she was unsure. Later, the police officer escorted us to the neighbor, who warmly welcomed us inside and ensured we were distracted with things to do. I sensed something was wrong, but I was unsure what it was and chose to stay quiet until our mother picked us up and drove us home. I do not remember when we were home. However, I did remember that our mother told the hearing sister first in private, and the sister was naturally heartbroken at that news. Then, she solemnly went to my bedroom, which I shared with my Deaf sister, to tell me the sad news that Sophia had passed away due to a heart attack in her sleep. I cried a lot because I understood her meaning and felt a heartbreaking loss. My family and I attended Sophia's funeral. We went out right before it was ready for burial. We witnessed John's love when he refused to leave the coffin and stayed with it until it entered a grave. That was one of my experiences of loss, and I wished that no one would experience that similar loss.

Nevertheless, I learned to appreciate the people around me and my family because I never knew if I would see them again the next day. That was a valuable yet undesirable lesson I must learn because we will lose someone we care about someday. We must remember that they live in our hearts forever. God knows, and He feels the loss as we feel on Earth. You may think that God is cold and unfeeling, but he did grieve the loss of his dear friends. In the Bible, ***"Jesus wept"*** when Mary, sister of Lazarus, told Jesus that Lazarus had passed away ***(John 11:35)***. Therefore, God has a range of emotions, and he empathizes with us when we experience different situations. It made us feel much closer to Him, didn't it? I know some people blame or question God for allowing tragic situations to happen, and comforting messages such as "God has a reason for that" are not very helpful to grieving people. You can show love like Jesus did: praying, bringing food, and asking what they can do to help the people in grief. People who grieve notice our ways of comfort and genuinely appreciate it. Sometimes words are not needed, and actions speak louder than words.

Moreover, the loss of loved ones through death is not the thing that sorrow, and regret will come together with; somebody may have experiences such as loss of friendship and relationships, painful feelings being apart from people you know in a place where you do not know anyone, sense of loneliness, and much more could be applied too. I had some regrets after feeling sorrow, but I realized that regrets are something we cannot fix. I gradually learned to let go, even if it was hard for me to do that, and I came out refreshed and slowly healed inside. It takes time, but resting and spending time with God to heal and lean on Him for support is worth it. I encourage you to do the same; your well-being comes first before you are ready to support and give energy to what matters to you.

Because of that, I understand that sorrow and regret always go together. It is inevitable, but we should not let the regrets drag us down but make us stronger, wiser, and more understanding. Life goes on, but we will never forget our memories and the feelings from specific experiences, for they live in our hearts. Suppose you know that regrets do not help but ooze negative emotions. In that case, you will address that by becoming a better person than before and doing things you will not regret.

6

Hope Gives Life to Anyone

"Hope is such a sweet sorrow and a bright light to one who seeks it."

Hope is the constant in my life because hope is the reason that saved my life many times. Hope has different meanings for everyone who lives for a long time on Earth, for they may see many things that give them a right to give up hope or life itself, but they choose to hold onto it. They may see death, wars, hunger, hatred, violence, fear, love, and many things, but they will agree that hope is why they live with a mindset to see to the end of their life.

Hope is the reason why I remain alive instead of ending my life in several attempts. Sometimes, I wouldn't say I like hope because my spirit stubbornly holds onto it while my body wants to give up. God knew and saw my struggles. He saw that I kept my hope to see Him in heaven someday and told me to hold onto it. When I was making my last attempt in a basement of my home during my junior year in high school, I felt that the Holy Spirit was telling me that God was here. He saw me in my painful struggle as I kneeled on the cold ground and held a knife to my heart. My mother and a few sisters were sleeping on the second floor, and they had no idea they might lose their family member that night. He told me He understood my struggle and assured me He was here. Then He gently spoke that it was not my time to die. It was hard to hear that, but I obeyed him and went to bed, sleeping and believing that things would improve as he promised. Writing this episode was tough because I never told everyone about this experience or how I decided to do it. Few friends and family members knew about my previous attempts. Even so, they did not know about this attempt because it was the last time, I decided to stop attempting suicide. Things did get better, as he promised, and I put my mental health first before others.

> ***And hope does not put us to shame, because God's love has been poured out into our hearts through the Holy Spirit, who has been given to us. (Romans 5:5)***

Thus, hope saved my life many times, so I look up at the sky, knowing God is looking back at me with a smile. Therefore, I remember to ***"be joyful in hope, patient in affliction, faithful in prayer" (Romans 12:12)***. I am putting the verses here so you can use them for your meditation and prayers for hope. It is a noteworthy cause for you to endure trials in life.

> ***For everything that was written in the past was written to teach us, so that through the endurance taught in the Scriptures and the encouragement they provide we might have hope. (Romans 15:4)***

This speaks of the stories in the Old Testament and New Testament that teaches us of their struggles and how they achieve victory in the name of putting their hope in God.

But blessed is the one who trusts in the Lord, whose confidence is in him. (Jeremiah 17:7)

That is the definition of Godly hope and entire trust that God will keep his promises and look out for us.

Yes, my soul, find rest in God; my hope comes from him. Truly he is my rock and my salvation; he is my fortress, I will not be shaken. (Psalm 62:5-6)

God is my rock and the reliable friend I can lean on for support and love. He never fails me ever -- even during my hard times.

That is why we labor and strive, because we have put our hope in the living God, who is the Savior of all people, and especially of those who believe. (1 Timothy 4:10)

That is a perfect summarization of why I live this life and remember that we are not working for the people, we are working for God.

And the God of all grace, who called you to his eternal glory in Christ, after you have suffered a little while, will himself restore you and make you strong, firm and steadfast. (1 Peter 5:10)

As he promised, he did make me stronger and wiser. I am more appreciative of life and stay rooted in my faith, which helped me to remain firm during unexpected moments and situations that may cause panic, worry, or fear. I am very thankful for these experiences that taught me not to be shaken by anything happening around me.

> ***But those who hope in the Lord will renew their strength. They will soar on wings like eagles; they will run and not grow weary, they will walk and not be faint" (Isaiah 40:31).***

That is a very encouraging and reassuring message that hope refreshes and strengthens us. Based on my experiences, I can verify this is true because I feel better when I declare that I put my hope in God. This message will help you when you are in challenging situations.

Lastly, I believe that ***"...our present sufferings are not worth comparing with the glory that will be revealed in us" (Romans 8:18)*** because Paul, the apostle, assured us in this verse that our sufferings are not for nothing. They meant to temper us through our sufferings so we can present our best self facing God the Lord. God confirmed that ***"...I have refined you, though not as silver; I have tested you in the furnace of affliction" (Isaiah 48:10)***. He provides trials and tribulations for us to get through to see if we make it through difficult situations or choose to give up and to forsake God for earthly things. We forget that God is eternal and temporal things are brief and eventually forgotten in time.

7

Life Is Beyond Our Control

*"Life is ever-changing and unapologetic.
Unbending to every human's whim. What can a
human do against life?"*

This phrase can be pessimistic; however, it is a fact that life is not full of glory and happiness as everyone expects. Life is meant to teach you something and have you experience ups and downs. It teaches you to take small steps instead of jumping to the next step. Sometimes you must step back to achieve a breakthrough before moving forward to see the results. Life will not go to whenever a person wishes to or grant a fairytale wish for them to get what they want instantly. It is something that we must work on with our hands and mind. God gives us the thinking brain, the functioning hands and legs to work on something that keeps us busy, and the sense of accomplishment when we finish a task or achieve a dream.

I have learned something after observing people and my working experiences; life is fairer to certain people and more unfair to others. Some people are born with a silver or golden spoon, but do they ask for that? No, it is not, and I know that some people envy these people for being born into rich or influential families. Nevertheless, we need to remember that we should not look over greener pastures and focus on what we have right now. Also, it is a fact that everyone is born into dysfunctional families, even wealthy or well-known families – even mine. We cannot deny that fact, but we can do something with what life has delivered to our doorsteps and make something good out of it. I had seen that people decided to cross to the greener pastures and were unhappier than before. So, I encourage you not to envy what other people have, and you will be glad that you do. God states this verse: ***"You desire but do not have, so you kill. You covet but you cannot get what you want, so you quarrel and fight. You do not have because you do not ask God (James 4:2)***. This is a good reminder and a warning to everyone tempted by envy to want something they should not act on because it will end in an awful conclusion no one wants to see. I also believe this other verse is something that you need to hear: ***"But if you harbor bitter envy and selfish ambition in your hearts, do not boast about it or deny the truth. Such "wisdom" does not come down from heaven but is earthly, unspiritual, demonic. For where you have envy and selfish ambition, there you find disorder and every evil practice" (James 3:14-16)***. You must avoid that if you feel envy or any selfish desires emerging in your heart.

Now, for my Deafhood – the positive term for Deafness – society and people immediately looked at Deafness negatively. They always chose to assume that Deafness means that person cannot do anything or more like they will not be successful in life. That is the stereotype and a wrongful assumption they commonly have toward Deaf people. Based on several experiences, I had a few Christians come to my friend while we were chatting at a restaurant or wherever; they told me that they would pray for my Deafness and handed me a brochure related to a church. I had to admit that I was surprised and secretly annoyed because I never thought it would happen to me; I did hear a few of my Deaf friends had this similar experience and did not think that it would also happen to me. My point is that I am proud of my Deaf identity, and I see there is nothing wrong with being Deaf at all. My Deafhood helped me to have an interesting perspective on the world and life and allowed me to appreciate my Deaf gains -- the advantages that hearing people do not have. It taught me to be more open-minded and contemplative. God even declares that I believe, in a nonchalant tone, ***"...Who gave human beings their mouths? Who makes them deaf or mute? Who gives them sight or makes them blind? Is it not I, the Lord?" (Exodus 4:11)*** to Moses. That remark was after Moses said he was not qualified to accept God's calling to go to Egypt to rescue Israelites and made an excuse that he was slow in speech and unskilled in communication skills. To me, it was a powerful realization that He gave me the gift of Deafness, and I considered it as my blessing.

I believe that wrongful assumption is the judgment they create when encountering a Deaf person. It is frustrating that they immediately make a judgment instead of remaining open-minded and seeing beyond the person's Deafness. People cannot judge people based on their actions, words, beliefs, or physical looks. For example, people had heard of the David and Goliath story. Still, not many people understand why God chose a humble shepherd boy, David, to be the king of the Israelites. There is a sort of parable for the reason why God chose David. In this story, the priest, Samuel, met with Jesse to see his seven sons, whom God decided to pick one of his sons to be the next king instead of King Saul. Samuel assumed that the first son brought in would be a king, but God told him to send in the remaining sons to pick the king. He told Samuel to ***"...not consider his appearance or height, for I have rejected him. The Lord does not look at the things people look at. People look at the outward appearance, but the Lord looks at the heart (1 Samuel 16:7)*** to show that God focuses on what is inside, not the external appearance. In the end, Jesse had to call David, who was herding the sheep, and God chose him immediately, for he was pleased with his love and obedience. Also, God hinted at David's identity as a shepherd boy. Metaphorically, Jesus Christ is like a shepherd leading the sheep to safety -- protecting them from Satan; he uses David's identity as a humble shepherd boy who later became a king in a similar analogy to Jesus Christ. God loves to show similar metaphors in the Old Testament that would happen or be mentioned again in the New Testament.

In some cultures, people believe that any physical defect is a punishment from God. It is inaccurate, and God intends to teach people something by telling them to look beyond a person's imperfections to see something extraordinary and be less judgmental that way. Ugliness has beauty, for I notice people always act kinder to good-looking people than ordinary or bad-looking people. Even scientific research proved it. My point is that God can use ordinary people, including the ones that society condemns or rejects, into extraordinary heroes in times of desperation, struggle, and hope to show that He can use us to glorify Him in marvelous ways. Despite his speech impediment, he uses Moses as an unexpected leader to deliver his glory to Egypt and the Israelites. My favorite story is the story of Rahab, the prostitute, because, in this biblical and even current timeline, people did not look favorably toward prostitutes and avoid them. However, God uses this remarkable woman to save the few Israelite spies from Jericho's king, who may capture and kill them. Only a few people realize that Rahab is the maternal ancestor of Jesus Christ! God did count Rahab's courageous behavior as righteousness -- saved by faith for her action to help God's chosen people in their time of need.

I am passionate about this because I am tired of seeing people make constant judgments every day. God only had a right to judge people, not us. Judgments cause more gossip, hearsay, lies, chaos, and confusion. God warned, ***"Do not judge, or you too will be judged. For in the same way you judge others, you will be judged, and with the measure you use, it will be measured to you"*** ***(Matthew 7:1-2)***. I am not ashamed to say that I sometimes judge others, but I catch myself afterward and strive not to judge others. After you read this chapter, you will also strive not to judge others but to treat others with gentleness and kindness. Please do not show pity but express your respect and support to people because they will appreciate that. Words can make a powerful impact if you use the correct words. I leave these two verses as a last thought for you all.

> ***I the Lord search the heart and examine the mind, to reward each person according to their conduct, according to what their deeds deserve. (Jeremiah 17-10)***

> ***You know when I sit down and when I rise up; You understand my thoughts from afar. You scrutinize my path and my lying down, And are intimately acquainted with all my ways. Even before there is a word on my tongue, Behold, O Lord, You know it all…Where can I go from your Spirit? Where can I flee from your presence? (Psalm 139:2-7)***

8

Life Sends Us Something

"Is life cruel? Yes and no. You are given a breath of life so you will have a taste of heaven and hell."

As I mentioned in Chapter 4, life on Earth is just a taste of what Heaven will be. Heaven is a paradise compared to Earth as a flower garden. God provides plants and animals for us to enjoy as food or companionship. We make food to celebrate different events such as the birth of a baby, a wedding, the end of a war, the reunion of friends/or family, etc. Yet, we also suffer from life affiliations such as bodily illnesses, wars, emotional entanglements, hard times, etc. We are here to appreciate life and enjoy what life provides us with additional blessings from God.

However, we grow to appreciate life even more when we suffer from various ailments and frustrations that make us look at life differently and with much wiser eyes. I recall that my adoptive mother remarked that I was a "zebra," and I asked what it meant. She said I had weird bodily illnesses that were random and unexpected compared to typical viruses, such as fever, flu, and allergies. I agreed since I like that term because I realized I had weird illnesses that plagued me when I was young. For instance, I had a strange feeling that something was inside my right thigh. My mother laughed and joked that she would take me to a hospital after I told her. She stopped laughing when she looked at my serious face when I stared at her when I was about 4-5 years old. She then took me to the hospital, and we sat in the waiting room until somebody called my name – I fell asleep before that – then I woke up lying on the hospital bed. I found the doctor and mother looking at me and speaking with each other. Later, they took me for an ultrasound test on my right thigh, and they surprisingly found a benign tumor! My mother was skeptical at first when I told her, but she was taken aback when she saw the screen showing the tumor. I had immediate surgery to remove it and became a happy and playful preschooler. Later, I had a few weird occurrences such as having surgery on my lip for a bump, a strange fever that lasted for 30-40 minutes quite in an abrupt manner after Sunday church attendance (preschooler), skin rashes that came and went (still have them to today), a sudden right leg paralysis for a day or two (2nd grader), and a chronic cough that lasts on and off still to today. I am also positive that I had some aftereffects of long Covid, yet I am still living well. What a rollercoaster of occurrences for me, indeed!

Yet, I praised the Lord for this life, for I learned to practice resilience, endurance, hope, and appreciation toward life no matter what life throws at me. I felt like Job in similar ways, for we suffered similar affiliations, and I empathize with him for I experience the same way. Regardless of that, I am truly blessed. Please look at these verses and think deeply about them.

For we brought nothing into the world, and we can take nothing out of it. But if we have food and clothing, we will be content with that. (1 Timothy 6:7-8)

I know what it is to be in need, and I know what it is to have plenty. I have learned the secret of being content in any and every situation, whether well fed or hungry, whether living in plenty or in want. (Philippians 4:12)

Since, then, you have been raised with Christ, set your hearts on things above, where Christ is, seated at the right hand of God. Set your mind on things above, not on earthly things. (Colossians 3:1-2)

9

Life and Death
are the
Lessons Themselves

"Hey, why must life and death cohabit? So that life and death cannot defeat each other for they are equal in the eye of the human."

Life and Death are important cycles for people to understand and accept, even though it is tough to know that Death will come for everyone. Life is essential because it symbolizes birth, hope, and joy, while Death is considered a final place of rest, fear of the unknown, and simply the end. People hold a significant interest in life because they want to take advantage of each moment to enjoy various pleasures before they die. Interestingly, people do not wish to discuss Death because it is something they cannot control, and they dislike knowing it. Besides, Death always gives unpleasant surprises to people who find that their loved ones or friends have passed away due to any factors. However, it is still heartbreaking to know someone passes away and never comes back. Death is such a finale, a conclusion that people cannot help but wonder where souls will go after Death. Many people will state that afterlife does not exist or there is heaven and hell after Death. God already explains that there is an afterlife after Death, only by accepting Jesus Christ as their way of salvation.

Jesus said to her, "I am the resurrection and the life. The one who believes in me will live, even though they die; and whoever lives by believing in me will never die. Do you believe this? (John 11:25-26)

I recognize life and death hold important roles and I did not fear them because I only knew that God is the master over them. I thought of this verse because it perfectly sums up how short our life is.

Show me, LORD, my life's end and the number of my days; let me know how fleeting my life is. You have made my days a mere handbreadth; the span of my years is as nothing before you. Everyone is but a breath, even those who seem secure. (Psalms 39:4-5)

I am glad I had a short life because it helped me appreciate my life more, pause, and look at beautiful sights around me. Everything on Earth belongs to Him, and everything inside me is His. My favorite pastime is looking up at the sky when it is blue and clear or dark as midnight, filled with stars and smiles, knowing God is looking at me and everyone on Earth. It is so incredible and mind-boggling that the people in the Bible like Moses, Abraham, Enoch, Elijah, Esther, Ruth, Mary (mother of Jesus), John the Baptist, and Jesus's first twelve disciples were also looking at the same sky that I am looking at right now. To me, death is just an invisible gate that opens to begin my new life, spending time with Jesus and other believers in Heaven. I am not afraid of death, but I fear pain. That is a weird statement, but that is my confession.

Nevertheless, I live a rich life full of trials, troubles, lessons, joys, realizations, spiritual experiences, and Christ-like endeavors. This life is a gift that God gave me, and I intend to fulfill my life by living a purposeful and Christ-like life. It is hard to have a deep self-awareness and handle everything around me. Still, it was worth discovering self-awareness and pursuing God in the race to the finish line. I consider death better because I can be with Jesus and walk with Him witnessing the great moments in the Second Coming and the Great Judgment. ***Philippians 1:23*** is closer to my ideal dream: ***"I am torn between the two: I desire to depart and be with Christ, which is better by far."***

10

God and Life Sees Everything We Do

"As the sun falls, silence reigns.
As the sun rises, sound roars."

What a rhythm in these poetic words above, right? You will agree that people often become busy during the day and rest at night. However, it may differ for some people who love to stay up at night for various reasons like reading books (that is me!), partying at clubs/bars, going to amusement parks, or watching a movie at theaters. So, it cannot be quiet sometimes at night too.

Still, this poetic phrase applies to working 9-5 people busy with work and daily errands; they can finally rest and relax at home. Work ethics are different for everyone. It is essential to know that you do your job and have some fun during the day and night while earning your keep to put the food on your table. The apostle, Paul, explained, **"For even when we were with you, we gave you this rule: 'The one who is unwilling to work shall not eat. We hear that some among you are idle and disruptive. They are not busy; they are busybodies. Such people we command and urge in the Lord Jesus Christ to settle down and earn the food they eat" (2 Thessalonians 3:10-12).** In other words, focus on your work and not let any problems in work get in your way or distract you by getting involved in gossip and negative talk. Getting involved in these kinds of discussions will not get you anywhere. Paul made this point to show how Christians should present themselves properly in the work environment, which will set an example for others to follow.

It is lively during the day and sometimes at night, mostly at weekends. However, some people choose to do the wrong things at night because they can do something in the dark where others cannot see them. Unfortunately, there is a belief that committing unacceptable stuff in the dark will not get you caught, or no one is watching you do things. However, God has something to say: ***"There is nothing concealed that will not be disclosed, or hidden that will not be made known. What you have said in the dark will be heard in the daylight, and what you have whispered in the ear in the inner rooms will be proclaimed from the roofs (Luke 12:2-3).***

Someone may not get caught committing things in the dark; however, many people forget that there is God who sees everything in the light and the dark. He knows what you are doing, even me, if I think no one is watching me. That is something that you need to think hard about, my friends. Is it worth doing something God is watching and may disapprove of your action? Think about it and try to live in the light. God promises that He ***"will bring every deed into judgment, including every hidden thing, whether it is good or evil"*** *(Ecclesiastes 12:14).*

Therefore, I advise you to live conscientiously and prudently even if you are a non-believer.

For Christians, please pause and think carefully about each action you take and think if God will approve it. I know that we are reborn again, but we sin too and ask for forgiveness from God. Please remind us that we should not sin for the same mistake. We are not perfect as people think we are due to the misconception about the born-again Christians who repent and are different from their previous sinful selves and free from sins. I am human, and I do make mistakes. Yes, I sin even though I am born again, but does it make God love me less or forsake me? No, He never abandons me. I need to remind myself to live for Christ and be a God-fearing person who thinks of God and does not focus on earthly things. Now, I leave you with several verses about darkness and light.

> ***To shine on those living in darkness   and in the shadow of death, to guide our feet into the path of peace. (Luke 1:79)***

> ***For our struggle is not against flesh and blood, but against the rulers, against the authorities, against the powers of this dark world and against the spiritual forces of evil in the heavenly realms. (Ephesians 6:12)***

> ***Woe to those who call evil good and good evil, who put darkness for light and light for darkness, who put bitter for sweet and sweet for bitter. (Isaiah 5:20)***

Even the darkness will not be dark to you; the night will shine like the day, for darkness is as light to you (Psalm 139:12)

11

The Meaning of Love

"What is love? It is more than romance, more than life, and more than dreams. It is a sweet, calm, and infinite warmth that refuses to give up, even in death."

Love endures for all ages, from the creation of the Earth to the present age. Love comes in different forms, but love is the foundation that is a glue to hold people in unity, hope, joy, and friendship.

God already proves His love through his Son, Jesus Christ, in this commonly heard verse around the world: ***"For God so loved the world that he gave his one and only Son, that whoever believes in him shall not perish but have eternal life" (John 3:16).*** Jesus died on the cross for our sins and to show His great love to us by showing that God does want us to be part of His family and to experience his blessings. This verse is so simple yet powerful that it sends the message to all people that God wants them to know that salvation is possible if only they believe deeply in their hearts and soul and that God loves them even in their imperfections, flaws, and mistakes.

God always shows His love in different stories aside from sending His Son, such as a story of Abraham's travels to find a home for his family, the Exodus from Egypt, and forty days in a wilderness for Israelites -- even during their rebellious periods and the worship of a golden calf, and money grubber-converted-believer, Zacchaeus (tax collector) who experienced condemnation and rejection by others. He even loves the Gentiles -- people that are not Jews -- by telling a Roman centurion that his servant had recovered after being impressed by the centurion's faith in his servants and belief that Jesus would heal his servant.

> **For I am not ashamed of the gospel, because it is the power of God that brings salvation to everyone who believes: first to the Jew, then to the Gentile. (Romans 1:16)**

> **Or is God the God of Jews only? Is he not the God of Gentiles too? Yes, of Gentiles too. (Romans 3:29)**

I have had experiences with love, even the unfortunate ones in my life. Jesus Christ was and still is my first love. In my embarrassing experiences when I was a very young 6th grader, I mistook infatuation for love. I apologize for the poor boys in my younger years. I acted like a love-struck fool and chased a few boys I had a crush on. Of course, all of them were hearing. I had a hardcore crush on one boy for a few years, and finally, I broke out of my rose-colored glasses when I saw that boy had had enough. After that, I learned to stay away from boys and remember to keep my feelings to myself if I had a crush on them during the rest of my school years. I gradually learn what romantic love is like, and romantic love works differently for everyone. For example, childhood friends grow up to become lovers, colleagues marry each other after being introduced by a mutual friend, or love at first sight for certain people in random places. Later, I had a few unsuccessful "almost relationships" with college boys at Gallaudet University. I learned from these lessons and decided to work on myself before getting ready to have a serious relationship where love is God-centered.

Looking back to my previous love experiences, I realized that I am looking to fill the missing parts inside of myself by putting myself in relationships hoping to get love from other people. These relationships taught me to love who I am and understand love requires mutual interest and effort from both parties. I realized that I was looking in the wrong places or people and that I should learn to appreciate who I am and improve myself first. Furthermore, I forgot or chose to ignore God, who is loving and unchangeable during these experiences. God proves He is always there and consistent with His love for me. He demonstrates his love by showing that He ***"...is the faithful God, keeping his covenant of love to a thousand generations of those who love him and keep his commandments" (Deuteronomy 7:9)***. He also added that nothing could stop him from loving all of us in this powerful verse: ***"for...that neither death nor life, neither angels nor demons,[a] neither the present nor the future, nor any powers, neither height nor depth, nor anything else in all creation, will be able to separate us from the love of God that is in Christ Jesus our Lord"***

(Romans 8:38-39). Therefore, I know love because God shows me how love works, like in friendships, family, colleagues, and pets. It is incredible and unfathomable that God knows our horrible mistakes and sees who we are but chooses to love us no matter what.

Love is a choice, not a feeling, because feelings change over time, but people keep choosing the same person they live with for a lifetime; that is love. You should look for the right person you can imagine living with for a lifetime. Let's continue to show love even to strangers and people in need because love brings great blessings that change people's lives. Love defeats everything, even in death, where Jesus rose from the dead, thus, saving us with his sacrificial love, giving hope and life to anyone who seeks Him.

> *And now these three remain: faith, hope and love. But the greatest of these is love. (1 Corinthians 13:13)*

> *Many waters cannot quench love; rivers cannot sweep it away. If one were to give all the wealth of one's house for love, it[a] would be utterly scorned. (Song of Solomon 8:7)*

> *The Lord appeared to us in the past,[a] saying: "I have loved you with an everlasting love; I have drawn you with unfailing kindness. (Jeremiah 31:3)*

> *You have heard that it was said, 'Love your neighbor[a] and hate your enemy.' But I tell you,*

love your enemies and pray for those who persecute you, (Matthew 5:43-44)

My poem:

Family

The love so pure, so sweet, that can be felt,
distinct and unconditional that it trumps fear.
Blood or not, it is the heart that matter, bonds that
hold friends and family together.

12

Peace Is the Goal in Life

"Peace," they say. What is peace? "I do not know," they answer. Then peace is unseen but felt in your soul, a calming force that dances to no one's tune."

People have their definitions of peace and tranquil environments. That is my definition of peace when contemplating life as I was on the metro heading to my internship in Washington, D.C., five years ago. My dream of a relaxed environment is to sit on the swinging chair with a book on my lap on the porch of my house overlooking a city with my dog and cat playing around on the grass with no disturbances and a beautiful cloudy blue sky above. That is my ideal and peaceful environment, and I want to turn that idea into a reality someday. I intend to live a quiet and peaceable life because life is chaotic around me often. Some people dislike peace because they need to move around and stay busy, which is okay. They are more comfortable doing something than sitting on a chair and doing some quiet entertainment. People have their preferences, including mine. I appreciate the silence and peace because I feel secure and calm. It helps me center myself and realign my mind to the right mindset.

In God's eyes, he encourages peace because hatred/evil has no place in his presence. He urged the believers to **"...turn from evil and do good; they must seek peace and pursue it" (1 Peter 3:11)**. You may agree that engaging in bad things would make life much messier than necessary, so that is why God knows and wants us to have peace amid the chaos around us. Paul explained that **"the mind governed by the flesh is death, but the mind governed by the Spirit is life and peace" (Romans 8:6)**. Thus, he means that we should let the Holy Spirit guides us and read Bible verses that bring life to our being instead of letting our heart desires and temptations lead us astray and getting lost in the dark, hence growing attached to our wants. It results in forgetting who we are since we are too deep into our obsessions and causes other messes to our loved ones' lives around us.

I know life can be overwhelming for all of us, and we wish for tranquility. We have moments of peace when we have restroom and office breaks from work, take a quick nap, or take a sick day off to relax and remove some stress and worries from our minds. It does help a lot. Mental health is crucial and always trending in the news because people are in a severe mental health crisis worldwide. We often forget our well-being because we have to work long hours to get money to pay for food on our tables and shelter over our heads, and that is not right to treat ourselves that way. I am thankful that Jesus Christ urged us to **"come to me, all you who are weary and burdened, and I will give you rest. Take my yoke upon you and learn from me, for I am gentle and humble in heart, and**

you will find rest for your souls. For my yoke is easy and my burden is light" (Matthew 11:28-30). I am delighted that I have Jesus to depend on when I feel life is challenging and stressful. He is willing to take some of my burdens to help me manage my everyday life better. Sometimes, I hide in my room for privacy and read quietly, thus enjoying the peace and silence away from the chaotic life.

But the fruit of the Spirit is love, joy, peace, forbearance, kindness, goodness, faithfulness, gentleness and self-control. Against such things there is no law. (Galatians 5:22-23)

13

Meaninglessness
Is Nothingness Itself

*"Describe the emptiness. A void of nothingness
and a sense of meaninglessness."*

I had plenty of meaningless experiences. The meaningless experiences include the feeling of emptiness inside your heart too. Most often, I will cover up my empty feelings inside by reading a book, sleeping, or taking a walk outside and looking at the greenery. It was not a pleasant feeling, but sometimes, we need to feel that to analyze why we sense that way and re-prioritize our life choices. I am sure many people try to cover up this feeling by taking drugs, drinking, partying, spending on a shopping spree, having sex or traveling to any place in the hope of feeling something. They do not realize that they are lost and need help. They feel something is missing in their hearts and think they need to do something to fill their emptiness. Sadly, many of them die or fall into deeper darkness from attempting to fill out the void. I had some meaningless experiences in which I would feel empty and tried to fill it up by eating something sweet, sleeping longer, or reading books. Nonetheless, they were not helping or helping a bit in a short time. When I sought the Bible to read some verses or pray to God, I felt much better and fuller in spirit.

"I once was lost, but now I'm found," these words sound familiar to you, don't they? These words are from *Amazing Grace*, one of my favorite lyrics to read and think about because this song always moves my heart and anyone who hears it. It is uplifting and full of hope. When I chose to believe in Christ as an eight or nine-year-old, I remember feeling something closer to an emptiness in my heart, muddling through life, and spending time getting to know my family. My mother took my sisters and me to the church in VA, McLean Bible Church, and she left my two Deaf sisters and me in a Deaf Sunday School classroom. One day, at an exact moment when my Deaf church teacher said something about what Jesus Christ did, I felt a spiritual calling in my heart. I leaped to my feet and signed aloud or whispered loudly in my heart, "**YES**" in answer to that call.

Afterward, I experienced several spiritual experiences where I knew God was talking to me. I did not regret giving my heart to Him every moment. One of these experiences was when I was praying while looking at the night sky through my room window and asking Him to send me a sign that He heard my prayers. Suddenly, I saw a quick flash of light in the mostly dark sky and a few stars. I was surprised when I saw it and felt deeply in my heart that it was Him answering my prayer, and I smiled, feeling assured that I was not alone. He was watching and always stayed around me even when I thought he was not there. It was a unique spiritual experience that I have always recalled. I remember that I completely adored Him for most of my childhood.

Later, I witnessed that He never failed to show me he was here with me by showing his presence in places that should be a coincidence, but I knew it was not a coincidence. He intended to show me that he was here paving a path for me and his sign that he never forgot me ever. I was lost, but I found my way to Him! Here are the verses on emptiness and advice from God about it.

Why spend money on what is not bread, and your labor on what does not satisfy? Listen, listen to me, and eat what is good, and you will delight in the richest of fare. (Isaiah 55:2)

Such is the destiny of all who forget God; so perishes the hope of the godless. What they trust in is fragile[a]; what they rely on is a spider's web. They lean on the web, but it gives way; they cling to it, but it does not hold. (Job 8:13-15)

14

You Exist for a Reason

"Wind exists; thus, you merely exist because you breathe, a proof that you exist."

As people leave quiet or loud footsteps when they come into life and leave their physical bodies when they leave the world, they existed long ago when we were not yet born and leave their traces behind to remind us of their existence. Our ancestors exist in history and our DNA, thus leaving proof that they lived and breathed like we do today. It was fascinating to know that people exist in separate times, but we would never meet them in our lifetime. That is why we see paintings or vintage portraits full of people we did not know, but we know that they lived in that period where they just lived, had feelings, and had the time of their life that we cannot see.

I love history because it was fascinating to see the people living during wars, doing their things, or simply enjoying their day with their loved ones. I confess that I wish I existed in the times of Abraham, Moses, Elijah, or most of all, Jesus because I want to be there to witness the biblical history of these people who have the personal conversation with God and prophets moving according to God's will to share His messages. I wished I was there to hear God's mighty voice and tremble in fear and awe as these biblical people and Israelites did. I was delighted that historical artifacts from archeological findings left the physical evidence that God and His people did exist according to the places stated in the Bible.

Certainly, God knew each of us, even those who had long gone ago. Imagine there are about one hundred seventeenth billion people from all periods, and He knew all of us. We barely know one hundred to two hundred people in our lifetime! King David even praised God in this song, ***"I praise you because I am fearfully and wonderfully made; your works are wonderful, I know that full well. My frame was not hidden from you when I was made in the secret place, when I was woven together in the depths of the earth. Your eyes saw my unformed body; all the days ordained for me were written in your book before one of them came to be. How precious to me are your thoughts, [a] God! How vast is the sum of them" (Psalm 139:14-17)!***

King David confirmed that God creates us thoughtfully and lovingly in his hands before we come to life inside our mother's womb. Thus, He knows us intimately and what we do in our lifetime! Isn't it amazing? I found this extraordinarily humbling and honored that God sees us from our embryo to our death. He was watching over each of us. Ultimately, we should make the most of our life, either for Him or ourselves. Here is some wisdom on the brevity of life:

Teach us to number our days, that we may gain a heart of wisdom. (Psalm 90:12)

Why, you do not even know what will happen tomorrow. What is your life? You are a mist that appears for a little while and then vanishes. Instead, you ought to say, "If it is the Lord's will, we will live and do this or that. (James 4:14-15)

Lord, you have been our dwelling place throughout all generations. Before the mountains were born or you brought forth the whole world, from everlasting to everlasting you are God. You turn people back to dust, saying, "Return to dust, you mortals." A thousand years in your sight are like a day that has just gone by, or like a watch in the night. Yet you sweep people away in the sleep of death — they are like the new grass of the morning: In the morning it springs up new, but by evening it is dry and withered. (Psalm 90:1-6)

My short poem about a brief life:

> *Ashes to ashes,*
> *Dust to dust,*
> *Return to the ground*
> *Where you lie.*
> *Sleeping for eternity.*

15

Loneliness Is a Path
That A Few Tread Onward

*"Loneliness is a sense of melancholy and a simple
contemplation of where you belong."*

I have dealt with loneliness for a long time, since I was young, due to being in hearing classrooms and being an outsider among my peers and sometimes my family members. Long ago, I would claim that loneliness was not a good feeling. Still, I grew to appreciate my solitary life because I found more peace than in social environments. I like my alone time a lot, so I can sometimes be irked if someone disturbs me. I consider myself a lone wolf because it perfectly describes me as solitary.

In the past, solitude contributed to one of the reasons I fell into a deep depression, and my Deafness worsened it. My Deafness automatically made me an outcast in the hearing classrooms. I dealt with that by bringing a book to read or chatting with a sign language interpreter to pass the time. I sometimes wished I was hearing to fit in and live an ordinary life. Hearing students did not know how to talk with me and were awkward, which was okay. We were teenagers, and we were getting to learn who we were. That was my regular school life. However, it was different in my college years.

It was a bit of an awkward and self-discovery journey during my first year, and I was thankful for the first friends I met. I joined the Honors Program because my mom told me there would be like-minded peers who could understand my level of intelligence and the desire for academic challenges. It was a great first two years of college life, even though I made some mistakes through that, and my mental health got better. However, I suddenly dropped into depression when some of my friends drifted off to make new friends, and I felt I was all over the place and needed a break for myself. Thus, I decided to withdraw and focus on my academics and myself for the latter two years. Then I recovered and returned to my feet to rejoin the social world again. Still, it was not the same since I felt that I did not have any friends who truly understood me or made an effort to deepen friendships with me. I put a lot of effort into companionship and did not get anything in return.

Therefore, I did what I knew best is to withdraw from social environments and focus on academics simply. Eventually, I went out alone to museums and restaurants. I treated myself to delicious sweets when I was in the mood. During this time, I started to analyze myself and discover my likes and dislikes. I enjoyed learning about myself again because I felt like I was a different self that I did not recognize due to my "rude person" experience that completely changed me. From that period of that experience to high school, I was a "walking zombie," and

I completely dissociated from my environment. I never smile or rarely do, and I keep a deadpan expression for a long time. Derealization was the term that I was feeling that way during that period. It was an unusual yet terrifying realization that I did not remember most of that period. If someone tells me about my experiences in that period, I cannot remember if I did this or that. Scientific research on depression found that memory loss is one of the aftereffects of depression. So that explains some of my memory loss. College years were when I rebuilt and discovered who I was, and still, to this day; I am learning more about myself every day. I finally learned to smile again during these college years and afterward. The growth mindset is something that I have been pursuing and striving to improve myself every day.

Even so, I am thankful for my single and solitary life because I found peace. I experienced hearing and deaf worlds, and I still felt out of place because deaf people sometimes do not get me. I just knew that I did not belong somewhere here on Earth. Jesus would understand me because he explained that "they are not of the world, even as I am not of it." (John 17:16) when he was praying to God the Father, speaking about the believers, including me. Peter also justified that by stating, "Dear friends, I urge you, as foreigners and exiles, to abstain from sinful desires, which wage war against your soul" (1 Peter 2:11). Foreigners are another word for strangers. I was an orphan and moved to Virginia when my mom adopted me in China at about three years old. You can say I was a stranger in my country for my Deafness and still considered a stranger in the U.S. due to my Asian skin and Deafness. Even Jesus agreed that he was a stranger and treated as an alien by his people too in his hometown, Nazareth. If you treat strangers with kindness, you show kindness and respect to people like Jesus Christ did. I leave this long verse for you to think about how to treat strangers thoughtfully.

> *For I was hungry and you gave me something to eat, I was thirsty and you gave me something to drink, I was a stranger and you invited me in, I needed clothes and you clothed me, I was sick and you looked after me, I was in prison and you came to visit me.*

> *Then the righteous will answer him, 'Lord, when did we see you hungry and feed you, or thirsty and give you something to drink? When did we see you a stranger and invite you in, or needing clothes and clothe you? When did we see you sick or in prison and go to visit you?'*

> *The King will reply, 'Truly I tell you, whatever you did for one of the least of these brothers and sisters of mine, you did for me.'*

> *Then he will say to those on his left, 'Depart from me, you who are cursed, into the eternal fire prepared for the devil and his angels. For I was hungry and you gave me nothing to eat, I was thirsty and you gave me nothing to drink, I was a stranger and you did not invite me in, I needed*

clothes and you did not clothe me, I was sick and in prison and you did not look after me.'

They also will answer, 'Lord, when did we see you hungry or thirsty or a stranger or needing clothes or sick or in prison, and did not help you?'

He will reply, 'Truly I tell you, whatever you did not do for one of the least of these, you did not do for me.'

Then they will go away to eternal punishment, but the righteous to eternal life. (Matthew 25:35-46)

16

You Are Beautiful As You Are

"When you are unapologetically yourself, you simply dazzle. That is beautiful."

As I mentioned in the chapter about humility teaches more than ego, I am in the middle of my self-discovery journey to understand myself and strive to be like Jesus Christ. I learned that focusing on God is better than worrying about what people think of me. Worrying about people thinking of me wastes my energy. It puts my mind into an unhealthy mindset where I try to please others and put myself last. Surely, Jesus and my younger self would be proud of me because I focus on growing and improving to be my best version. Indeed, putting myself in the right mindset is worth my time and energy. I strive to think positively and lend a listening ear when someone needs to talk, thus passing the calm energy to others. I also learn how to work on my boundaries and communicate in better, clear, and kind ways to others so they can return it with respect. Looking back, I was in awe and grateful that God truly worked hard inside me to be a version that I like and want to be, contrary to my previous self, who was gloomy, introverted, and emotionally stunted. Some people commented that I was better and more pleasant than before, and I knew why I had changed for the better. I thought of this verse that perfectly describes how I feel about improving myself. I am sure you may like to hear this too: ***"But he said to me, "My grace is sufficient for you, for my power is made perfect in weakness." Therefore I will boast all the more gladly about my weaknesses, so that Christ's power may rest on me. That is why, for Christ's sake, I delight in weaknesses, in insults, in hardships, in persecutions, in difficulties. For when I am weak, then I am strong" (2 Corinthians 12:9-10).*** I am thankful for the good and bad times, good experiences, and lessons that make me who I am today with the guidance of God in my life.

Therefore, I urge you, my friends, to recognize and learn more about yourselves so you can better serve and give uplifting energy to others, thus spreading much kinder humanity around. I firmly believe people are beautiful when they are just themselves rather than someone they want to be, not realizing that being themselves will draw the right people who will be their support if they just let themselves be. Pleasing others will certainly not result in good outcomes because people only care about their benefits more than they care for other people, and you may lose your identity in this process. It is normal to do that, but humanity will always be there, which is good. As Paul asked in his writings, ***"Am I now trying to win the approval of human beings, or of God? Or am I trying to please people? If I were still trying to please people, I would not be a servant of Christ" (Galatians 1:10).*** Now, my question is, are you willing enough to abandon who you are to be someone that you think that everyone wants you to be and end up unhappy and depressed or being yourself and know your worth and values, thus finding the right people who will stay in your life and live a much fuller life? I would pick the latter if I were you, but it is yours and everyone else's choice. I had lived a life of the former, and I dare to say that I did not miss that period because I muddled my way around and looked foolish while doing that. Must I remind you that you only have one life, a precious blessing? So, live the life you choose and live with that decision with no excuses.

You may wonder how to be yourself in the chaotic and noisy world. I may have an answer, but it is one of many answers you may want to consider regarding how to live your life. Based on my experiences growing up and thinking about life almost every day, I learned that I must always center on one or a few things that define me and stay with it, thus making my roots stronger, facing the storms of life coming my way or around me. I learned to know my core values and hobbies that define me best. As I indicated in my foreword page, the three values that were important to me and part of my identity are faith, open-mindedness, and a growth mindset. Faith is the anchor of my lifeline and why I aim to see my end as God has seen. At the same time, open-mindedness is the opportunity to grow wiser and more understanding and not hold something against life. A growth mindset is helping me to move forward and enjoy every present moment, thus healing inside and recognizing that everyone is different and moving at a different pace in life. I sincerely hope and pray that this advice helps someone find themselves or use that to guide their life forward in the direction they wish to walk.

Now faith is confidence in what we hope for and assurance about what we do not see. (Hebrews 11:1)

Trust in the Lord with all your heart and lean not on your own understanding; in all your ways submit to him, and he will make your paths straight. (Proverbs 3:5-6)

Do not conform to the pattern of this world, but be transformed by the renewing of your mind. Then you will be able to test and approve what God's will is—his good, pleasing and perfect will. (Romans 12:2)

17

We May Struggle with Our Demons but Light Heals Us

"Why does darkness fear the light? Because light will drive away the demons."

This phrase could mean in a literal or metaphorical sense. In the literal interpretation, I am sure that some of you like to watch thrillers and horror films (me too!) and root for people to fight through terrifying situations and come out victorious and alive. It feels good to see these survivors fight through the horrors and not let the fear get them as they get closer to the light and safety. The killers or ghosts will disappear or avoid sunlight because the darkness enables them to move fearlessly, knowing the survivors cannot see them in the dark. At the same time, light obstructs them from doing that. I also think that you may hear or see similar situations related to demon possession. In one Bible story, Jesus was driving a demon called the "Legion" out of a man they possessed. Surprisingly, the demons pleaded in fear begging Jesus not to torture them after He commanded the demons to get out of that man. Then Jesus permitted them to go to a herd of pigs after demons asked Him not to send them out of the area *(Mark 5:1-13)*.

This situation showed that demon spirits fear Jesus Christ and recognize Him immediately. They knew that He was God in human form. Isn't it interesting that demons knew who He was despite Jesus not revealing who He was to the Israelites and His twelve disciples yet? I know that you may hear horror stories when you see things moving or being thrown across the room when spirits/demons hear the name of Jesus Christ. It is clear that they fear and hate Him, but they cannot do anything to Him, so they are just expressing their anger by doing these things.

This situation certainly brought me to mind that I do not understand why people still firmly believe that Jesus Christ is just a "good man," "prophet," or "saint" while simply saying "Jesus Christ" to these spirits/demons, and they immediately fear that name. These same people will speak that name to exorcize demons and spirits even though they do not believe in Him. Clearly, it shows that Jesus Christ is a mighty person to me. If I do not know who He is, I will wonder why hearing His name terrifies demons. Demons had no fear toward humans and animals, even angels. Still, they are intimidated by powerful spiritual beings like Jesus Christ that they cannot defeat or are powerless against Him. Previously, demons were the angels created by God, so it is as clear as a day that God still has power over them even after they fell from grace (Heaven) for taking Satan's side.

To put it plainly, <u>Jesus is God</u> based on these few verses: ***"In the beginning was the Word, and the Word was with God, and the Word was God" (John 1:1)*** and

"The Word became flesh and made his dwelling among us. We have seen his glory, the glory of the one and only Son, who came from the Father, full of grace and truth" (John 1:14).

Finally, Jesus Christ has a few mighty titles added to His name that includes <u>God</u>: ***"For to us a child is born, to us a son is given, and the government will be on his shoulders. And he will be called Wonderful Counselor, Mighty God, Everlasting Father, Prince of Peace" (Isaiah 9:6).*** Will you dare to refute that fact Jesus is not God even when demons believe it? Look at that verse, ***James 2:19***, and tell me if you can deny that. To me, Jesus Christ represents light, for He did declare that He is ***"the light of the world. Whoever follows me will never walk in darkness, but will have the light of life" (John 8:12).*** Demons fled from his presence. Even Satan could not tempt him with worldly desires when he wandered in the wilderness for forty days using God's words to counter Satan's tests.

On the other hand, in the metaphorical sense, light represents hope, love, warmth, and safety. In contrast, darkness represents fear, despair, hopelessness, and loss. We could view demons as our internal and external struggles, and we may look for "light" in things that may help us to deal with our conflicts. However, the "light" we look at is not the actual light but rather the comforting addictions that allow us to manage our demons for a short time. For example, people may struggle with mental health and physical pain or hold much bitterness. They may turn to drugs, alcohol, partying, doing shopping sprees, or sex so they will not feel the demons that hound them. Sadly, many people are doing that now; it is nothing new. Believe it or not, the authentic "light" they are looking for is:

- Human connections

- Support from their communities and therapy

- Activities that help them to heal and reconnect to themselves again

I had some experiences with my demons – depression, the feeling of unworthiness, and resentment – and I turned to my comforting addictions: sleeping, reading novels, and sometimes going on a shopping spree. However, do these soothing addictions help me at all? Not at all. They only helped to ease some of my discomforts and assisted me in forgetting my troubles for a short time. Then my demons returned, reminding me I could not avoid them forever. Finally, I chose to fight my demons by facing them and recognizing them for what they are. Then, I ask God in prayers to help me work on my demons and heal internally. I prayed long and hard for this many times and found myself getting better and slowly letting go of things that I should not dwell on; thanks to the spiritual strength He provides.

Reading some of my favorite chapters, such as Psalms and Proverbs, helped me immensely. I started to connect with these Bible characters, such as David, Elijah, Job, and Esther, because I saw some of myself in them. David made some horrible mistakes, but He truly loves God. Elijah experienced deep depression, but He still obeyed

God no matter what. Job suffered many physical and emotional pains but never lost faith in God. Esther was a mysterious yet brave woman when she put her God's chosen people first before her life as she faced the powerful king-husband to save her people. These biblical characters and I are flawed, broken, sometimes disobedient, and imperfect human beings. God uses us as He transforms our mistakes and flaws into something greater with much grace. Therefore, His grace is enough to cover our faults and broken selves and to teach us that broken things would transform into something beautiful and life changing. Paul explained, ***"my grace is sufficient for you, for my power is made perfect in weakness. Therefore I will boast all the more gladly about my weaknesses, so that Christ's power may rest on me" (2 Corinthians 12:9).*** The chapter about *being beautiful as you are be* mentioned this verse too.

Nevertheless, it is the verse that we need to affirm every day because we must proudly acknowledge that we are imperfect and flawed beings. Still, with God's help, we would be better. King David perfectly described God as the light in His life and mine. I hope this verse refreshes you and guides you to enlightenment too.

> ***The Lord is my light and my salvation — whom shall I fear?***

> ***The Lord is the stronghold of my life — of whom shall I be afraid?***

When the wicked advance against me to devour[a] me, it is my enemies and my foes who will stumble and fall.

Though an army besiege me, my heart will not fear; though war break out against me, even then I will be confident. (Psalm 27:1-3)

18

I See You

"A person may have or be many things. If you want to truly understand and connect with them, see beyond their images and truly see them for themselves. That is where the connection happens. 'I see you' are the magic words. In other words, to understand is great, but to be understood and be seen is marvelous and powerful."

To be seen for who we are is very important and meaningful to us. You will agree that connection forms when you truly know someone for themselves and accept who they are despite their flaws and imperfections. You have parents, friends, and colleagues who see a few or some of yourselves you allow. You find that you may make some lifelong friendships that last forever or a lesson that you see them for who they are despite the claims they say they are. Connection is when you look at their eyes and see the vulnerable self they may try to hide or show fearlessly behind their facade. You find that you want to learn more about them and love them harder than when you both met. It is an irresistible feeling at that moment that you may experience the times when you meet people in everyday life. It was a rare but precious feeling when you felt a deep connection beyond the physical encounter. For example, think of the story of an enslaved person, Hagrid, who was mistreated and pregnant with Abraham's son by Sarai, the wife of Abraham, and fled from her to a well in a desert. Later, an Angel of the Lord appeared and inquired why she was there at the well, and she responded that she was fleeing from Sarai. The angel told her to go back, and she obeyed, stating that ***"You are the God who sees me,"*** and went back as told *(Genesis 16:13)*. This statement shows how powerful the feeling of being seen and understood as Hagar has proclaimed with such certainty and reassurance that God recognized her for who she is, minus her identity as a bondswoman. Imagine the feeling that she thought no one cared about her. Still, God appeared to her immediately and assured her that He did care, ignoring her origins – Egyptian and bondservant. Speaking of that, she might never expect a holy and omnipresent being to appear to her, a humble and insignificant person, to tell her such simple yet compelling sentences that gave back her confidence and a memory that she would never forget in her lifetime. It was rare that God would appear to anyone – it could be counted on two hands – but whatever He did, you will be sure that He did that for a reason and to teach people reading the Bible to understand that He genuinely sees and cares for each of us. That is why He loves to listen to our prayers and rantings because He wants us to come to Him as who we are, and He will eagerly make a connection with us.

I recalled the scene in a movie called Avatar: The Way of Water, where Jake Sally finally understood his son, Lo'ak, and told him, "I see you," after their previous tense relationship and misunderstandings. This simple sentence was used as a greeting in Pandora and can mean two things. One meaning is "I see you" in a physical form of respect, and the second is that I understand you spiritually. I believe that Jake said both things when he spoke to Lo'ak. For Hagar to feel that God recognized her in a desert and spiritually comforted her, which strengthened her to return and submit to her mistress, Sarai, again. I also perceive "I see you" as **I love you** statement, so God essentially told Hagar that too. Perhaps, Hagar felt unloved and invisible after being used as a surrogate mother.

While on the subject of "I see you," another Bible story deeply moved me and caused me to admire a particular person very much. She was and is still my role model. Ruth was her name, a Moabite, one of the tribes God told the Israelites not to intermarry with because this tribe was a pagan nation. Anyway, Ruth was one of the daughters-in-law of Naomi, the Israelite. Naomi and daughters-in-law experienced profound loss by losing their husbands. Naomi decided to send the daughters-in-law back to their tribes so they could remarry again. Ruth refused while another daughter-in-law, Oprah, went back to her hometown. Ruth then said that wonderful declaration to Naomi that notably moved me, ***"Don't urge me to leave you or to turn back from you. Where you go I will go, and where you stay I will stay. Your***

people will be my people and your God my God. Where you die I will die, and there I will be buried. May the Lord deal with me, be it ever so severely, if even death separates you and me" (Ruth 1:16-17). We honestly had no idea what happened in the life of Ruth that caused her to pronounce that. Despite that, we could infer that she saw something in her husband and Noami's belief in God that led her to make that vow. This wonderful and moving vow declared that she wanted to stay with Naomi. She implied that she now sees God as her God, thus removing her previous beliefs and everything she ever knew to accept the new faith. Therefore, we could assume that God heard her declaration and saw her loyal devotion to Naomi. Because of that, He blessed her by sending Boaz, a man of God, to be her husband. Naomi saw the blessing God bestowed her, the grandson Obed, and knew that God did not forsake her and gave her renewed strength, thanks to Ruth.

Ruth was one of the few chapters that spoke about female heroes, specifically Ruth, honoring her for her loyalty, diligence, and kindness. Even Ruth earned her place as a maternal ancestor of Jesus Christ too! She was blessed to be part of Jesus Christ's genealogy, thus proving that God could look beyond people's flaws and identities and use them for His greater purpose.

The Epilogue

"I write for no one knows their ending, not mine, but only God knows. I only know my life is written by Him."

My life was in His hands when I chose to follow Jesus. Do I regret that choice? No, it was a tremendous privilege and an honor to get to know Jesus and what He had done for everyone, including me. I am very blessed to know Him and have that deep desire to chase Him to heaven, where He awaits. I long for my ending than my day of birth, for I knew I would see more incredible things if I was in His presence than being on Earth with him unseen, walking with me on the path he created. Still, it is a privilege to have Him guide me and help me have more profound realizations as I walk through my short life.

On the land I walk on, this land belongs to Him; he creates the sky I look at; the water I swim through, He provides to sustain us. What more can I say to prove that He exists everywhere? You cannot see your breath in the air or know where the wind goes? These things that you cannot see but know exist, so why do you question whether God exists? If God does not exist, what makes us humans, Earth, and everything in it? I will think you stupid if you claim aliens make us because even aliens look at us as strange creatures. Hence it means they do not recognize us. I will see you as a fool if you believe we come from nothingness. If so, why do we exist, and where will we go after we die? To nothingness? Then everything will be meaningless, and our existence will be futile too. Do you prefer realizing that you are here for nothing or feeling that you are here for a reason in a spiritual sense?

As far as I see, people like to be Somebody rather than Nobody, so I leave you to wonder with these questions I posed and think about your life. Perhaps you may have a change of heart and want to talk with God, do it, and see what He will do in your life then.

I conclude this with a thought, can you claim that God is not real? If so, then show me the proof that He does not exist. I encourage you to watch the movie series "God's Not Dead" and tell me if you still believe God is not real. For some reason, people like to see things happening before their eyes, thus forgetting that God is Holy and superior to their weak human bodies. I know that people demand to see God in person. God is everywhere, wherever he pleases on Earth and Heaven, and He freely can decide if He wants to appear to anyone in person. So, must He respond to their insolent demand? Still, Jesus heard that similar demand when people demanded Him to come down from the cross and mocked that if He was God as he claimed, He should miraculously come down. Jesus chose not to perform that easy miracle because He knew humans would find excuses to justify their human reasonings if he came down from the cross, hence making God's plan worthless. God's goal is to reconcile and save us from Death, which we rightly deserve due to our sins, thus giving us a choice to follow Jesus as our Way, the

Life, and the Truth, or reject Him to pursue worldly things and pleasures.

I am the Alpha and the Omega, the First and the Last, the Beginning and the End. (Revelation 22:13)

This is what the Lord says — Israel's King and Redeemer, the Lord Almighty: I am the first and I am the last; apart from me there is no God. (Isaiah 44:6)

Afterword

Dear readers,

I hope you found this book refreshing and eye-opening to understand my perspective on life and what God has done. I pray that wherever you are, you leave with some gains gleaning from this book and pass it on to someone you think should read it.

I challenge you to think about your life and to see if God has his hands moving your path. God moved people according to His plan despite them thinking they decided to pioneer their way forward. There is a reason you meet certain people in your life. Think of what they have taught you or leave something for you to realize when they depart. Perhaps you can consider God's hands in your life. To me, coincidences are something that atheists or non-spiritual people will use as an excuse to explain preposterous situations. However, these coincidences are God's intent to tell me why I am there, and He is working behind the scenes to move me from place to place. It is not fate or the universe as people claim to explain why things happen. It is God truly.

Lastly, can you all do me a favor? Please do not curse using these words, "Jesus Christ" or "Oh my Lord/God," if you do not believe in God, then why bother to use these words for curses? If someone asks you not to curse in front of them, then please respect them. Thank you very much.

I consider this book my letter to God and readers alike. God is my first reader since He saw what I wrote before this book was published. I am writing this book to put my thoughts into paper, expressing some of my contemplation on life and God.

God, thank you for everything truly. I do not regret my life here because you help me see what I need to see and understand what you are trying to tell me spiritually. The memory of being saved through Jesus Christ is something that I will never forget since it was precious and considered a phenomenal treasure worth much more than mere money or everything I own here on Earth. Amen.

God bless you all!

Farewell,
Angela Rogers

For more information contact:

Advantage Books
info@advbooks.com

To purchase additional copies of these books, visit our bookstore
at www.advbookstore.com

Orlando, Florida, USA
"we bring dreams to life"™
www.advbookstore.com

www.ingramcontent.com/pod-product-compliance
Lightning Source LLC
Chambersburg PA
CBHW071455030726
47593CB00003B/1010